Juniper Networks Certified Data Centre, Professional (JNCIP-DC) Exam Practice Questions & Dumps

Exam Study Guide for Juniper Networks (JN0-681) Exam Prep Latest Version

Presented by: Quantic Books

About Quantic Books:

Quantic Books is a publishing house based in Princeton, New Jersey, USA., a platform that is accessible online as well as locally, which gives power to educational content, erudite collection, poetry & many other book genres. We make it easy for writers & authors to get their books designed, published, promoted, and sell professionally on worldwide scale with eBook + Print distribution. Quantic Books is now distributing books worldwide.

Note: Find answers of the questions at the last of the book.

QUESTION 1
You are designing a Layer 3 fabric underlay using EBGP. You will implement an EVPN-signaled VXLAN overlay on the Layer 3 fabric.
In this scenario, what must you do in the underlay to ensure that the VXLAN overlay will be able to function properly?

A. The underlay should advertise the host-connected interfaces on all leaf devices.
B. Each device in the underlay should advertise its loopback address.
C. The underlay should be configured with a separate VRF for each potential tenant.
D. The underlay should support the PIM protocol.

QUESTION 2
You are configuring VXLAN, and you must ensure that all switches for the

multicast groups advertise their existence and learn about other VTEPs. In

this scenario, which protocol will accomplish this task?

A. OSPF
B. BGP
C. EVPN
D. PIM

QUESTION 3
You work in a data center where VMs and hosts are frequently moved. Your

design needs to eliminate inefficient traffic flows. In this scenario, which two

solutions will satisfy this requirement? (Choose two.)

A. VXLAN
B. EVPN
C. VMTO
D. VPLS

QUESTION 4
You host a multitenant data center that runs VMware. You must perform deep packet inspection on all inter-tenant traffic that is flowing between the VMs within the same hypervisor. Your solution must provide the security services without needing to leave the physical device.

In this scenario, what should you do to solve this problem?

A. Use separate vSwitches to isolate each tenant's networks and use IP tables to evaluate inter-tenant traffic.
B. Use VLANs to isolate each tenant's networks and use an SRX Series device to evaluate inter-tenant traffic.
C. Use a vMX device to isolate each tenant's networks and use with firewall filters to evaluate inter-tenant traffic.
D. Use separate vSwitches to isolate each tenant's networks and use a vSRX Series device to evaluate inter-tenant traffic.

QUESTION 5
You are configuring an EVPN overlay network. You want to ensure that leaf devices can respond to ARP requests from locally connected hosts, when the leaf

device knows the MAC of the intended destination.

In this scenario, what should you configure on the leaf devices to accomplish this task?

A. proxy ARP
B. static ARP entries
C. persistent MAC learning
D. IGMP snooping

QUESTION 6
Which two statements describe MAC address learning for VPLS and EVPN? (Choose two.)

A. EVPN learns MAC addresses in the data plane.
B. VPLS learns MAC addresses in the control plane.
C. VPLS learns MAC addresses in the data plane.
D. EVPN learns MAC addresses in the control plane.

QUESTION 7

A company wants to expand their hosting business and is seeking solutions to support multiple tenants. Each tenant should be able to configure their own logical interfaces. Also, based on customer needs, all routing features must be supported.
What will satisfy the customer's requirements?

A. routing instances
B. tenant systems
C. logical systems
D. bridge domains

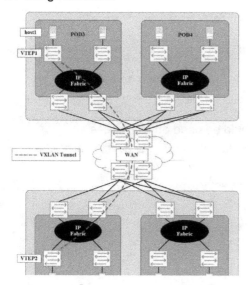

QUESTION 8

After configuring an IP fabric using EBGP as your routing protocol, you notice that not all of the routes are showing up in the routing tables. You have verified that all adjacencies have formed, and that all policies are in place and configured properly.
In this scenario, which statement is true?

A. The routers have not been configured with the `multipath multiple-as` parameter.
B. The routers have not been configured using the `add-path` parameter.
C. The routers have not been configured using the `bfd-liveness-detection` parameter.
D. The routers have not been configured using the `multihop` parameter.

QUESTION 9
Referring to the exhibit, DC1 and DC2 have a DCI across a service provider WAN connection. Host1 in DC1 must have Layer 2 connectivity to host2 in DC2. A VXLAN tunnel must be created between VTEP1 and VTEP2. In this scenario, which statement is true?

A. The service provider WAN connection cannot be an MPLS-based WAN connection.
B. VXLAN Layer 3 gateway must be provisioned at the Super Spine layer.
C. A route to the loopback address on VTEP2 must be present on VTEP1.
D. VTEP1 and VTEP2 must peer using IBGP.

QUESTION 10
You are designing an EBGP IP fabric for a multi-site data center.In this

scenario, which two statements are true? (Choose two.)

A. Public AS numbers must be used.
B. Different AS numbers should be used on all devices.
C. The same AS number should be used on all devices across all data centers.
D. Private AS numbers can be used.

QUESTION 11

An EVPN-signaled VXLAN overlay has been deployed in the network shown in the exhibit. Host1 is a bare metal server, and is dual-homed to the network. The IP addresses 10.1.1.1/24 and 10.1.1.2/24 are assigned to the same physical NIC, and no virtualization is configured on the server.

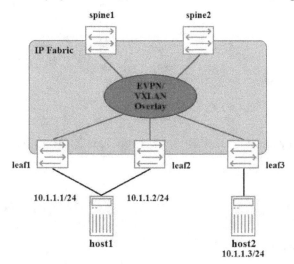

In this scenario, which two statements are true? (Choose two.)

A. The MAC address associated with 10.1.1.1/24 and 10.1.1.2/24 will be the same when advertised to leaf3.

B. The connection from host1 to devices leaf1 and leaf2 must be configured as a LAG.

C. Traffic from IP address 10.1.1.1/24 must traverse the VXLAN network to reach IP address 10.1.1.2/24.

D. The ESI assigned to the leaf1-host1 link must be the same as the ESI assigned to the leaf2-hostl link.

QUESTION 12

You are implementing perimeter security for your data center. You need to inspect all traffic at Layer 7 and ensure the failure of a port or device will not result in an interruption to traffic flows.
In this scenario, which design would satisfy these requirements?

A. SRX using LAG

B. MX with MC-LAG

C. QFX Virtual Chassis

D. SRX chassis cluster

QUESTION 13
In the exhibit, VM1 is part of the same VXLAN segment as VM3.

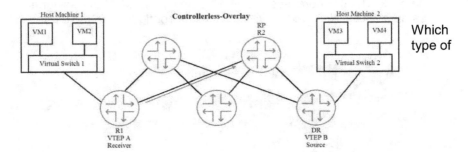

Which type of

message will R1 initially send to R2 so that VM1 receives BUM traffic from VM3?

A. IGMP Join (S,G)
B. PIM Join
C. IGMP Join (*,G)
D. PIM Register message

QUESTION 14
You are asked to design a deployment plan for a large number of QFX Series switches using ZTP. The ZTP deployment plan must ensure all switches are configured with their designated configuration file.

Which DHCP option and suboption combination would be used to accomplish this task?

A. DHCP option 43 with a suboption of 00
B. DHCP option 66 with a suboption of 00
C. DHCP option 66 with a suboption of 01
D. DHCP option 43 with a suboption of 01

QUESTION 15

You are asked to deploy 20 QFX Series devices using ZTP. Each QFX5100 requires a specific FTP server.In this scenario, which two components must you configure on the DHCP server? (Choose two.)

A. the IP address of the FTP server

B. the MAC address of the FTP server

C. the IP address of each QFX5100

D. the MAC address of each QFX5100

```
user@switch> show route 10.1.2.0/24

inet.0: 11 destinations, 13 routes (11 active,
holddown, 0 hidden)
+ = Active Route, - = Last Active, * = Both

10.1.2.0/24          *[BGP/170] 01:21:05,
localpref 100
                      AS path: 64516 I,
validation-state: unverified
                      to 172.16.3.1 via ge-
0/0/1.0
                      > to 172.16.5.1 via ge-
0/0/2.0
                      [BGP/170] 01:09:08,
localpref 100
                      AS path: 64515 I,
validation-state: unverified
                      > to 172.16.3.1 via ge-
0/0/1.0

user@switch> show route forwarding-table
destination 10.1.2.0/24
Routing table: default.inet
Internet:
Destination         Type RtRef Next hop
         Type Index    NhRef Netif
10.1.2.0/24           user     0 172.16.5.1
         ucst      574      4 ge-0/0/2.0
...
```

QUESTION 16
You are configuring an IP Fabric in your data center and you are trying to load-balance traffic across multiple equal-cost BGP routes. You have enabled multipath, but the traffic is not being load-balanced.

Referring to the exhibit, what will solve this problem?

A. You should apply the `load-balance` policy as an import policy to the forwarding table.
B. You should apply the `load-balance` policy as an import policy for the BGP neighbor.
C. You should apply the `load-balance` policy as an export policy to the forwarding table.
D. You should apply the `load-balance` policy as an export policy to the BGP neighbor.

QUESTION 17
When using EBGP as the underlay protocol for your IP fabric architecture, which two statements are true? (Choose two.)

A. Spine nodes only peer to leaf nodes.
B. Leaf nodes peer to both spine and leaf nodes.
C. Leaf nodes only peer to spine nodes.
D. Spine nodes peer to both leaf and spine nodes.

QUESTION 18
What are three advantages of using MPLS for data center interconnects? (Choose three.)

A. dedicated MPLS backbones for Layer 2 and Layer 3 DCIs
B. any-to-any connectivity
C. traffic engineering
D. dedicated connections between customer sites
E. sub 50 ms failover times

QUESTION 19

You have configured a new MC-LAG connection to a host. After committing the configuration, the MC-LAG link is not functioning properly.

```
{master:0}[edit interfaces ae1]           {master:0}[edit interfaces ae1]
user@gfx1# show                           user@gfx2# show
aggregated-ether-options {                aggregated-ether-options {
    lacp {                                    lacp {
        active;                                   active;
        system-id 01:01:01:01:01:01;              system-id 01:01:01:01:01:01;
        admin-key 1;                              admin-key 1;
    }                                         }
    mc-ae {                                   mc-ae {
        mc-ae-id 0;                               mc-ae-id 1;
        chassis-id 0;                             chassis-id 1;
        mode active-active;                       mode active-active;
        status-control active;                    status-control standby;
    }                                         }
}                                         }
unit 0 {                                  unit 0 {
    family ethernet-switching {               family ethernet-switching {
        vlan {                                    vlan {
            members v15;                              members v15;
        }                                         }
    }                                         }
}                                         }
```

Referring to the exhibit, how would you solve this problem?

A. Change the `chassis-id` on qfx1 to 1.
B. Configure a `system-id` on qfx1 that is different from the `system-id` on qfx2.
C. Configure the `status-control` on qfx2 to active.
D. Change the `mc-ae-id` on qfx1 to 1.

QUESTION 20

Which two combinations are supported when configuring a Virtual Chassis Fabric? (Choose two.)

A. two spine nodes and 28 leaf nodes
B. four spine nodes and 20 leaf nodes
C. four spine nodes with 16 leaf nodes
D. two spine nodes and 16 leaf nodes

QUESTION 21

The MC-LAG group shown in the exhibit is providing high availability services for the directly connected servers. The backup liveness detection is applied to the ICL- PL link, however, when one of the members rebooted, there was traffic loss for a few seconds.

In this scenario, where should you apply the backup liveness detection?

A. on the ae1 interface
B. on the ae2 interface
C. on the management interfaces
D. on the ae0 interface

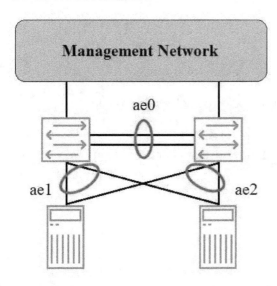

QUESTION 22

Which two statements define the use of route targets and route distinguishers in an EVPN? (Choose two.)

A. Route targets ensure that routes from different clients remain unique within the data center domain.
B. Route targets identify the VRF into which the route should be placed.
C. Route distinguishers ensure that routes from different clients remain unique within the data center domain.
D. Route distinguishers identify the VRF into which the route should be placed.

QUESTION 23

You are asked to enable plug-and-play for future line card switches in an active VCF without making any future Junos configuration changes. You are also required to ensure that all new line cards are automatically upgraded to the correct Junos version without any manual intervention.

In this scenario, which two actions will accomplish this task? (Choose two.)

A. Ensure that the newly inserted line card's MAC addresses are present in the DHCP configuration for ZTP.
B. Configure the `auto-sw-update` parameter on the VCF before inserting new line cards.
C. Set the Virtual Chassis as pre-provisioned before the line cards are inserted.
D. Set the Virtual Chassis as auto-provisioned before the line cards are inserted.

QUESTION 24

A VXLAN has been created between devices leaf1 and leaf3.

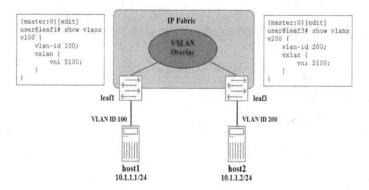

Referring to the exhibit, which statement is true?

A. Traffic sent from host1 to host2 will be tagged with VLAN ID 200 when exiting leaf3.
B. Traffic sent from leaf1 to host2 will he dropped on leaf1.
C. Traffic sent from host1 to host2 will be tagged with VLAN ID 100 when exiting leaf3.
D. Traffic sent from leaf1 to host2 will he dropped on leaf3.

QUESTION 25
What is the endpoint of a VXLAN tunnel?

A. DLCI
B. VTEP
C. LSR
D. VCF

QUESTION 26
Which EVPN route type prevents BUM traffic from looping back to a multihomed host?

A. IP prefix route
B. Ethernet autodiscovery route
C. Ethernet segment route
D. inclusive multicast-Ethernet tag route

QUESTION 27
You have a site with thousands of MAC addresses multihomed to two leaf nodes in an EVPN VXLAN.

In this scenario, which EVPN feature provides fast network convergence in the event of a leaf node link failure?

A. BGP Additional Paths
B. Bidirectional Forwarding Detection
C. Ethernet Autodiscovery
D. Fast reroute

QUESTION 28
What are two methods used to scale an IBGP IP Fabric? (Choose two.)

A. spanning tree
B. redundant trunk groups
C. route reflection
D. confederations

QUESTION 29

Which protocol is used between VCF member devices to create a loop-free topology?

A. LLDP
B. MSTP
C. RSTP
D. VCCP

QUESTION 30

You have deployed a VXLAN as shown in the exhibit Leaf1, leaf3, spine1, and spine2 have been configured as VTEPs. Host1 cannot communicate with host2.

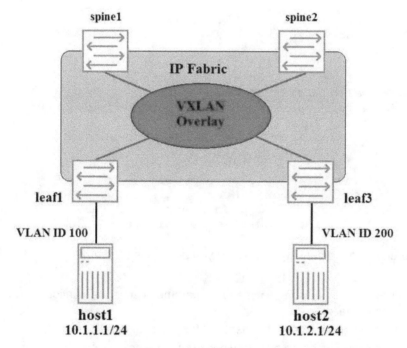

Referring to the exhibit, how would you solve this problem?

A. The VLAN ID on the link connected to host2 must be changed to VLAN 100.
B. A DCI connection must be created between the VLANs.
C. A Layer 3 VXLAN gateway must be configured on at least one of the devices.
D. Host1 and host2 must be placed in the same VRF.

QUESTION 31

You have configured MP-IBGP to support EVPN for your overlay network. However, you are not seeing the expected routes on your edge devices.

```
Peer: 10.255.14.182+179 AS 69      Local:
10.255.14.176+2131 AS 69
   Type: Internal     State: Established       Flags:
<ImportEval>
   Last State: OpenConfirm    Last Event:
RecvKeepAlive
   Last Error: None
   Options: <Preference LocalAddress HoldTime
GracefulRestart AddressFamily     Rib-group
Refresh>
   Address families configured: inet-vpn-unicast
evpn
   Local Address: 10.255.14.176 Holdtime: 90
Preference: 170
   Number of flaps: 0
   Peer ID: 10.255.14.182     Local ID:
10.255.14.176    Active Holdtime: 90
   Keepalive Interval: 30
   NLRI for restart configured on peer: inet-vpn-
unicast l2vpn
   NLRI advertised by peer: inet-vpn-unicast
l2 vpn
   NLRI for this session: inet-vpn-unicast
   Peer supports Refresh capability (2)
   Restart time configured on the peer: 120
   Stale routes from peer are kept for: 300
   Restart time requested by this peer: 120
```

Referring to the exhibit, how would you solve this problem?

A. The `family evpn signaling` parameter must be configured on the remote peer.

B. Graceful restart must be disabled for this session.

C. The group types on both devices should be set to `external`.

D. The family `l2vpn signaling` must be configured on the local peer.

QUESTION 32
Your manager asks you to secure ARP and DHCP traffic across your local

Ethernet links.In this scenario, which technology will accomplish this task?

A. SSL
B. a firewall filter
C. IPsec
D. MACsec

ANSWERS

1. Correct Answer: B
2. Correct Answer: C
3. Correct Answer: AB
4. Correct Answer: D
5. Correct Answer: A
6. Correct Answer: CD
7. Correct Answer: A
8. Correct Answer: D
9. Correct Answer: C
10. Correct Answer: BD
11. Correct Answer: BD
12. Correct Answer: D
13. Correct Answer: B
14. Correct Answer: A
15. Correct Answer: AD
16. Correct Answer: C
17. Correct Answer: AC
18. Correct Answer: ACE
19. Correct Answer: D
20. Correct Answer: CD
21. Correct Answer: C
22. Correct Answer: BC
23. Correct Answer: BD
24. Correct Answer: A
25. Correct Answer: B
26. Correct Answer: B
27. Correct Answer: C

28. **Correct Answer: CD**
29. **Correct Answer: D**
30. **Correct Answer: C**
31. **Correct Answer: A**
32. **Correct Answer: D**